GIRLS playing SPORTS
Coloring Book

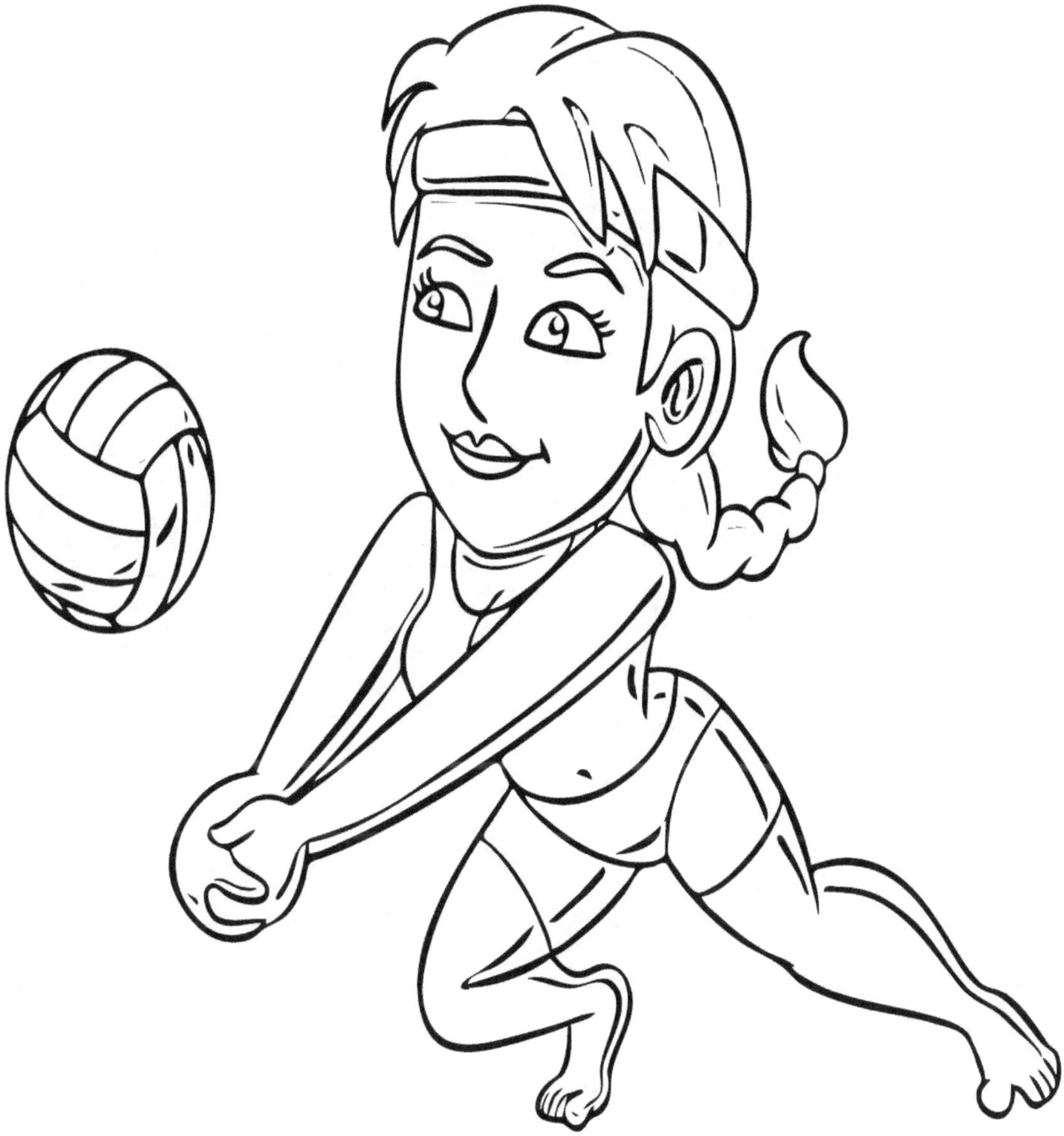

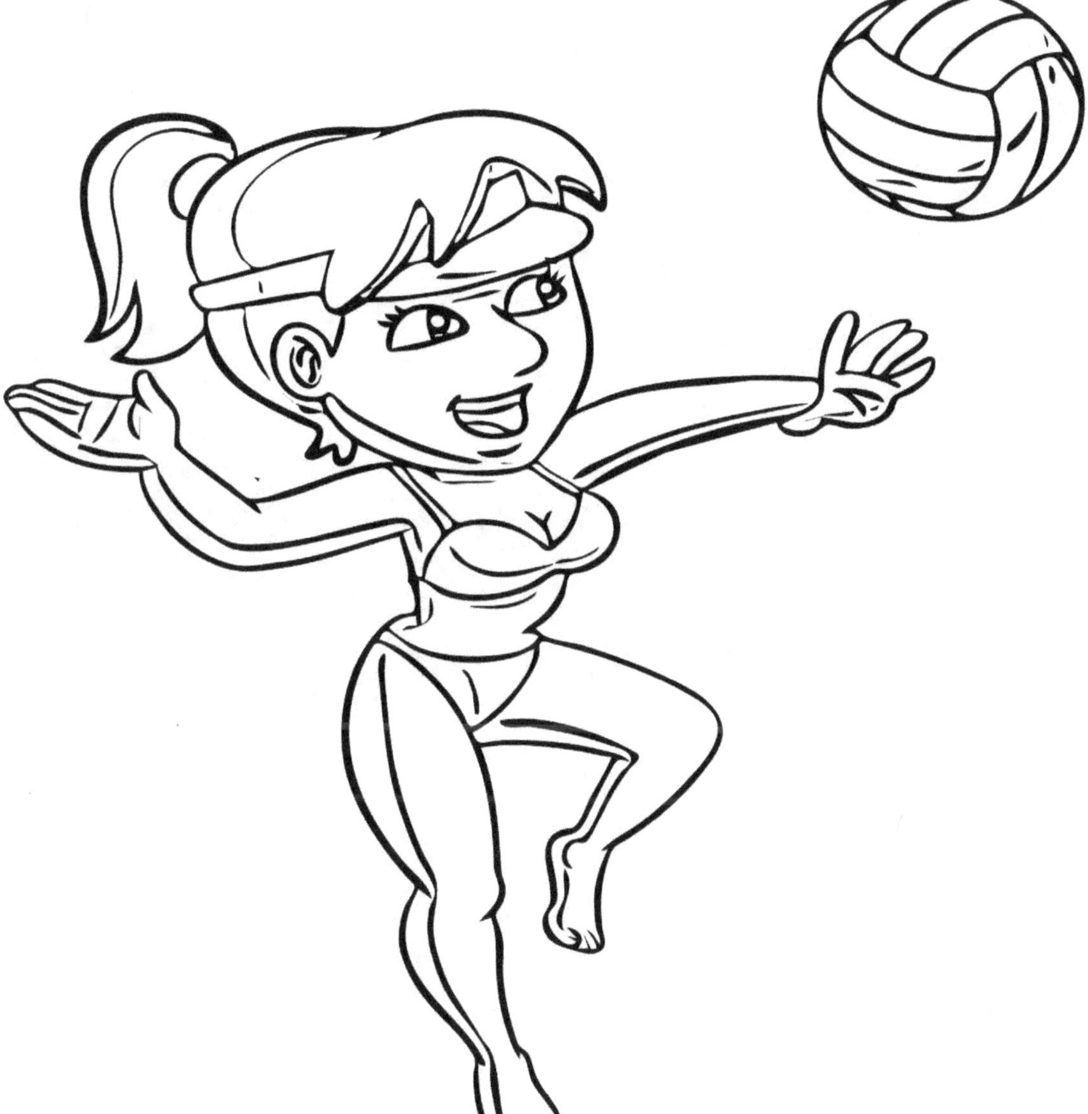

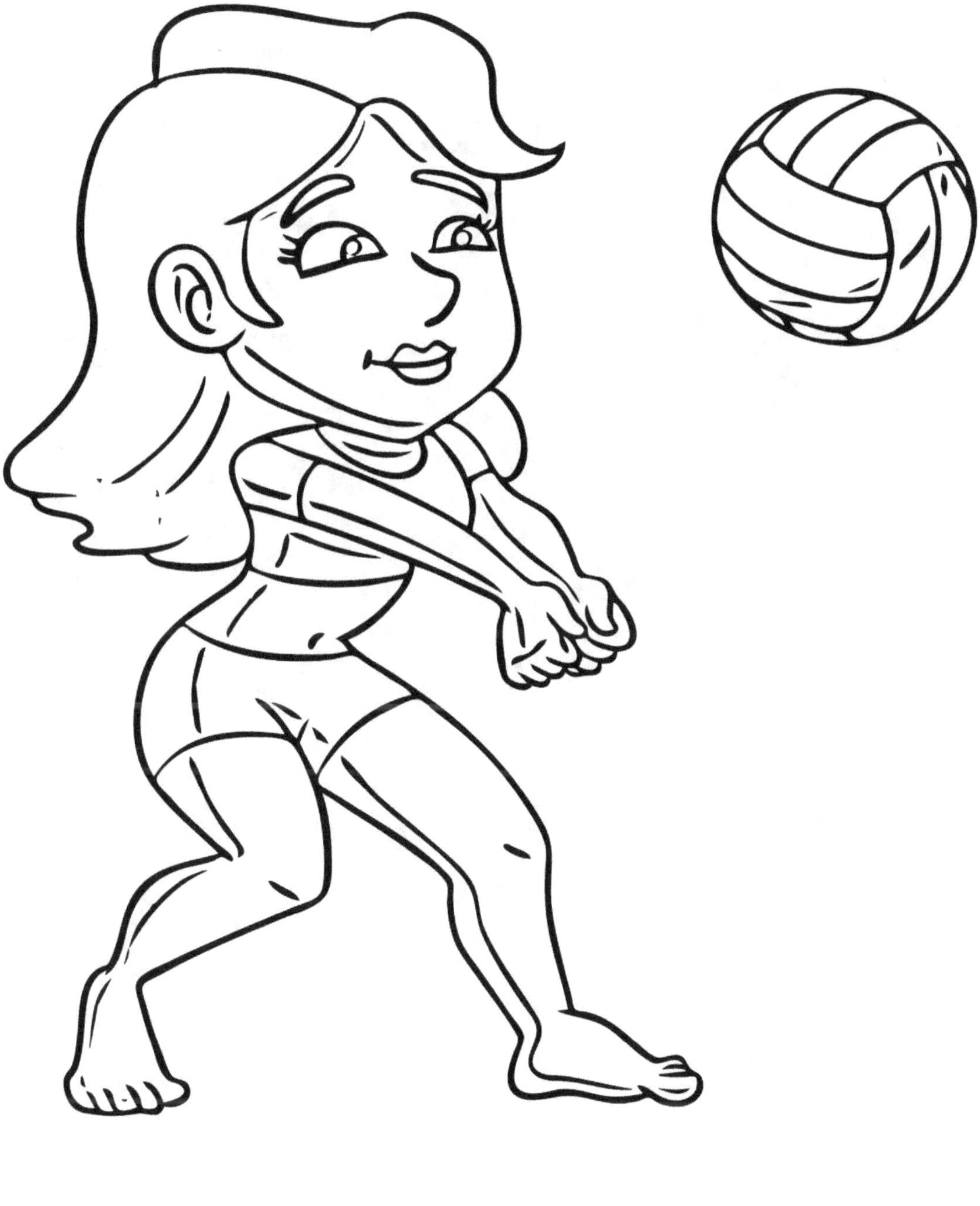

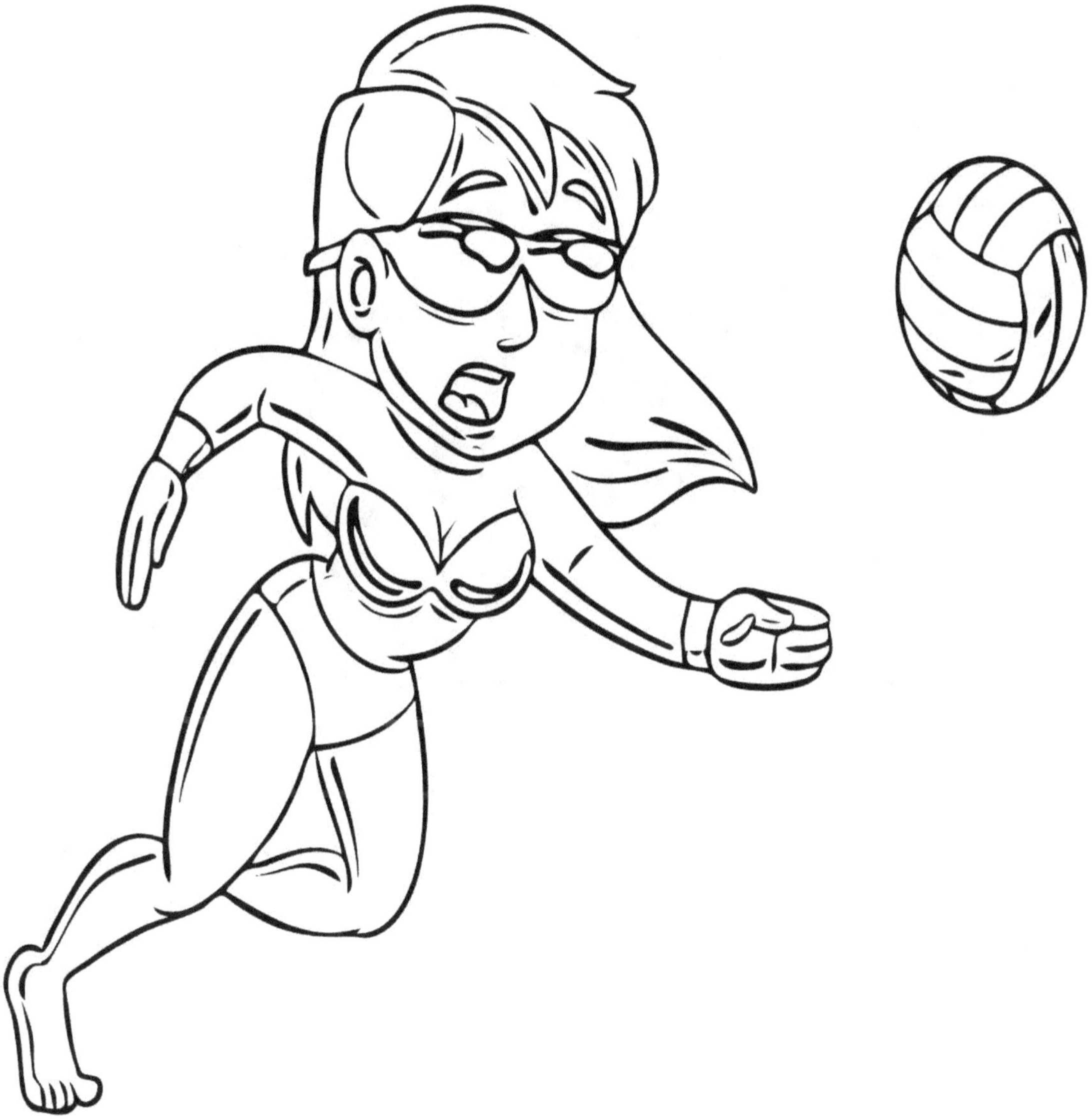

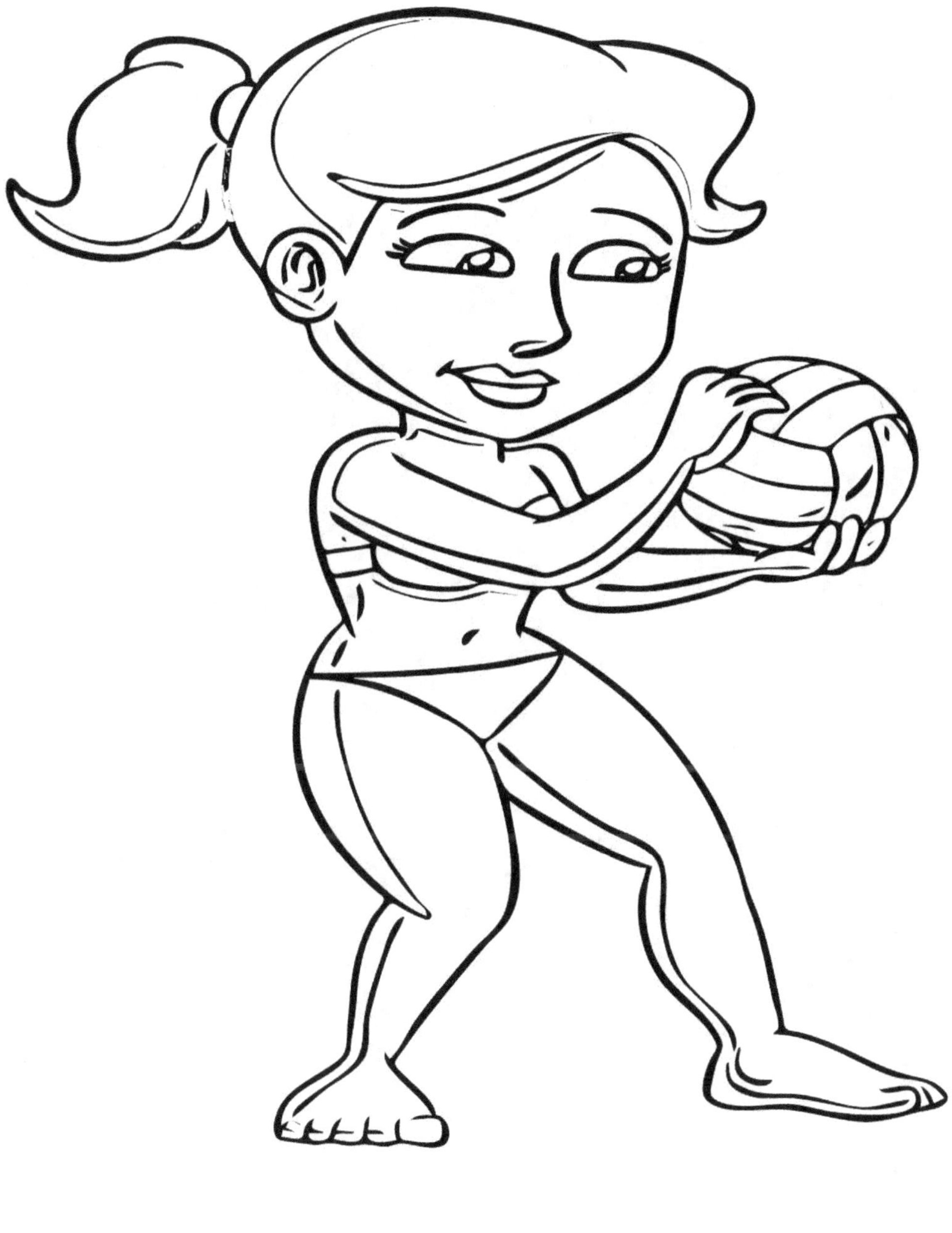

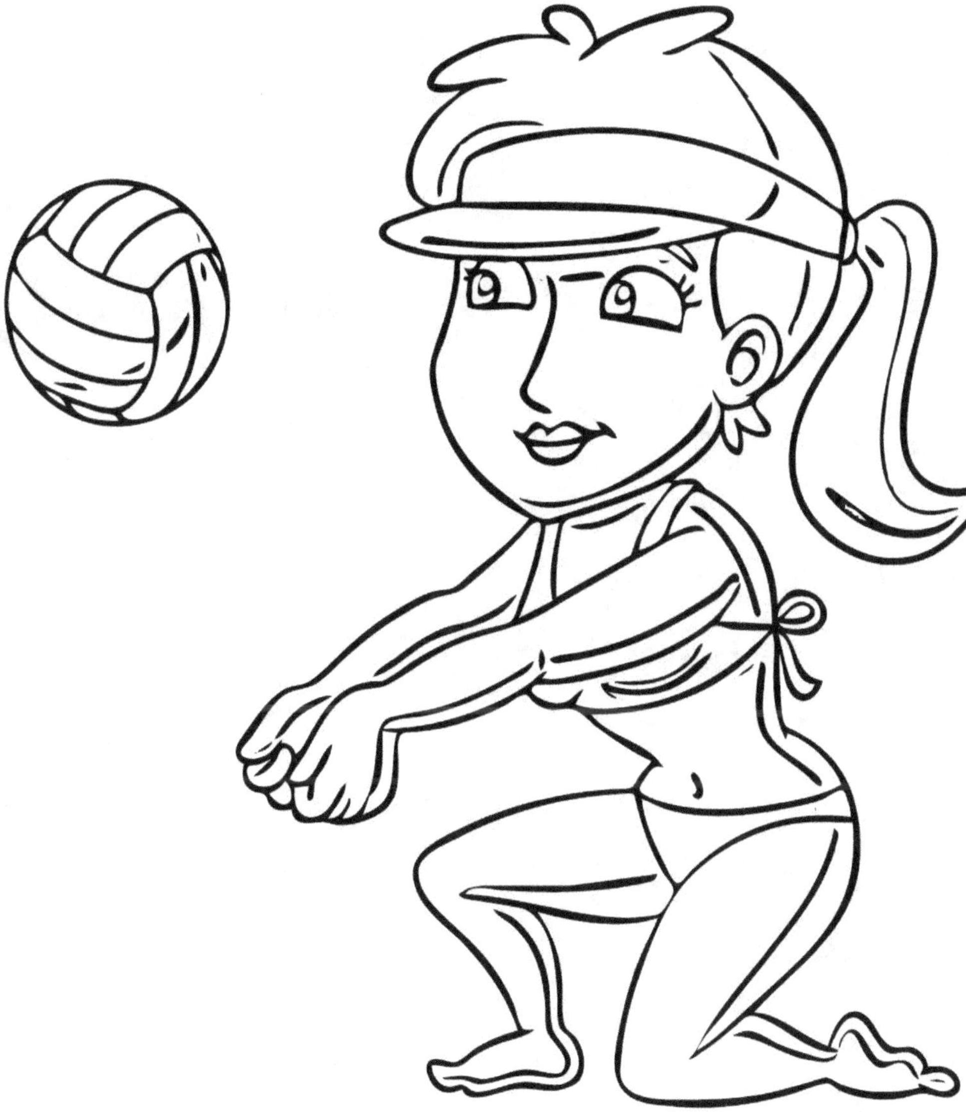

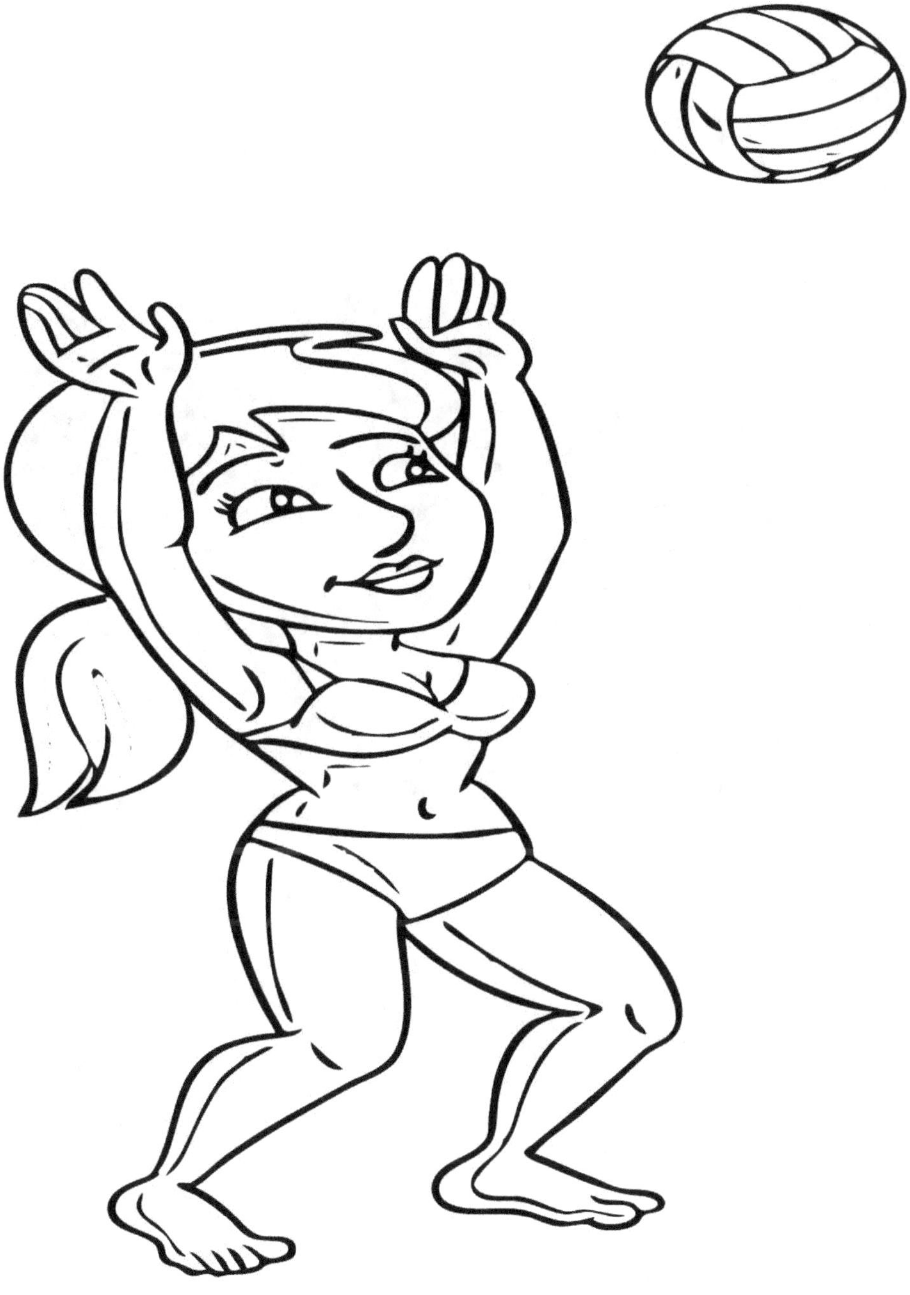

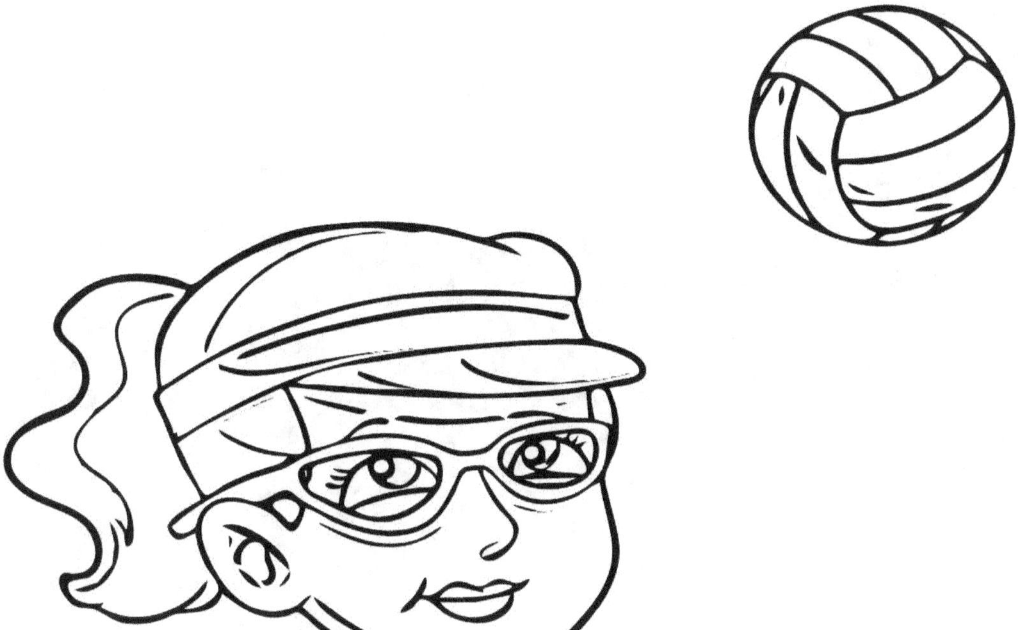

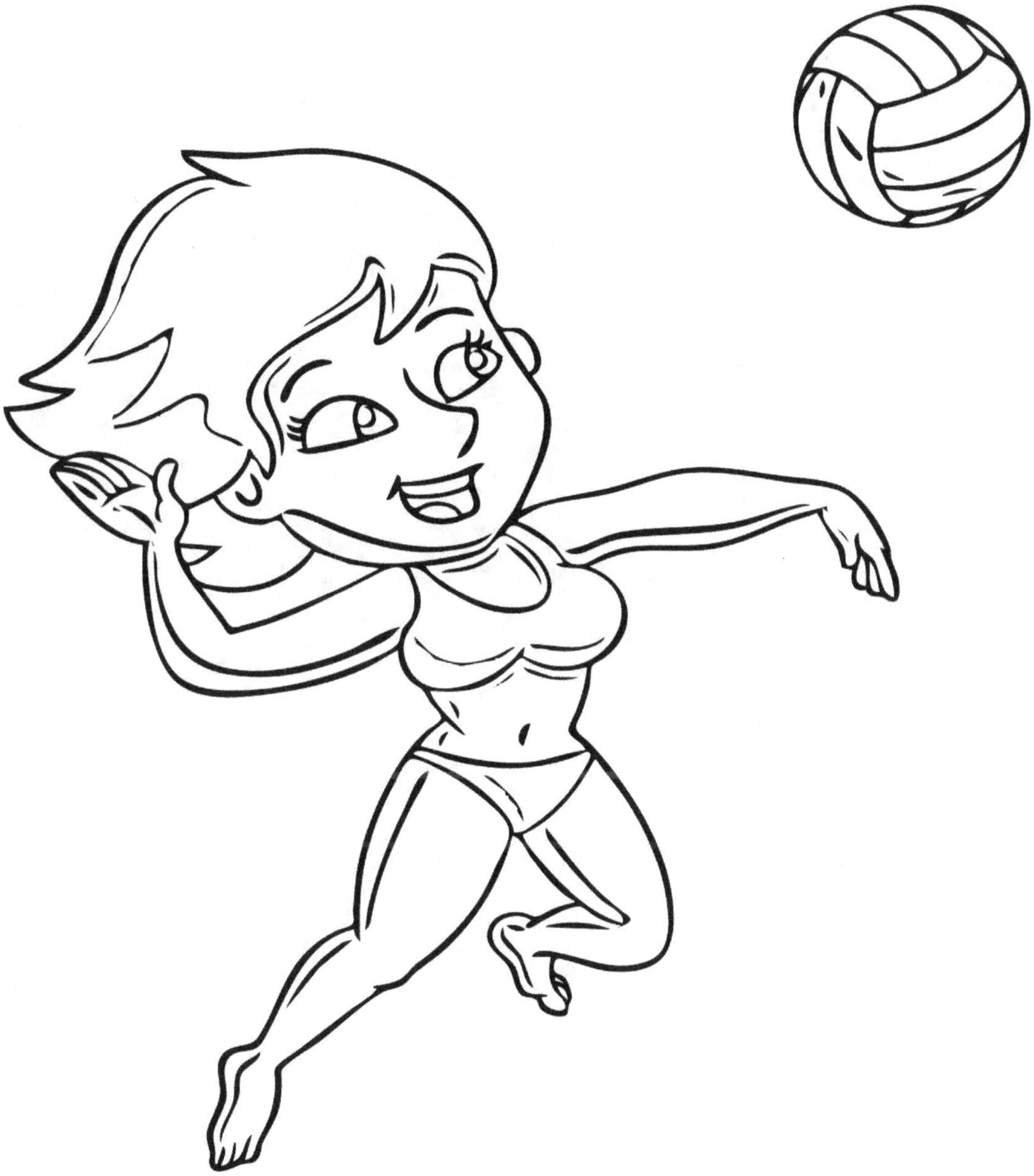

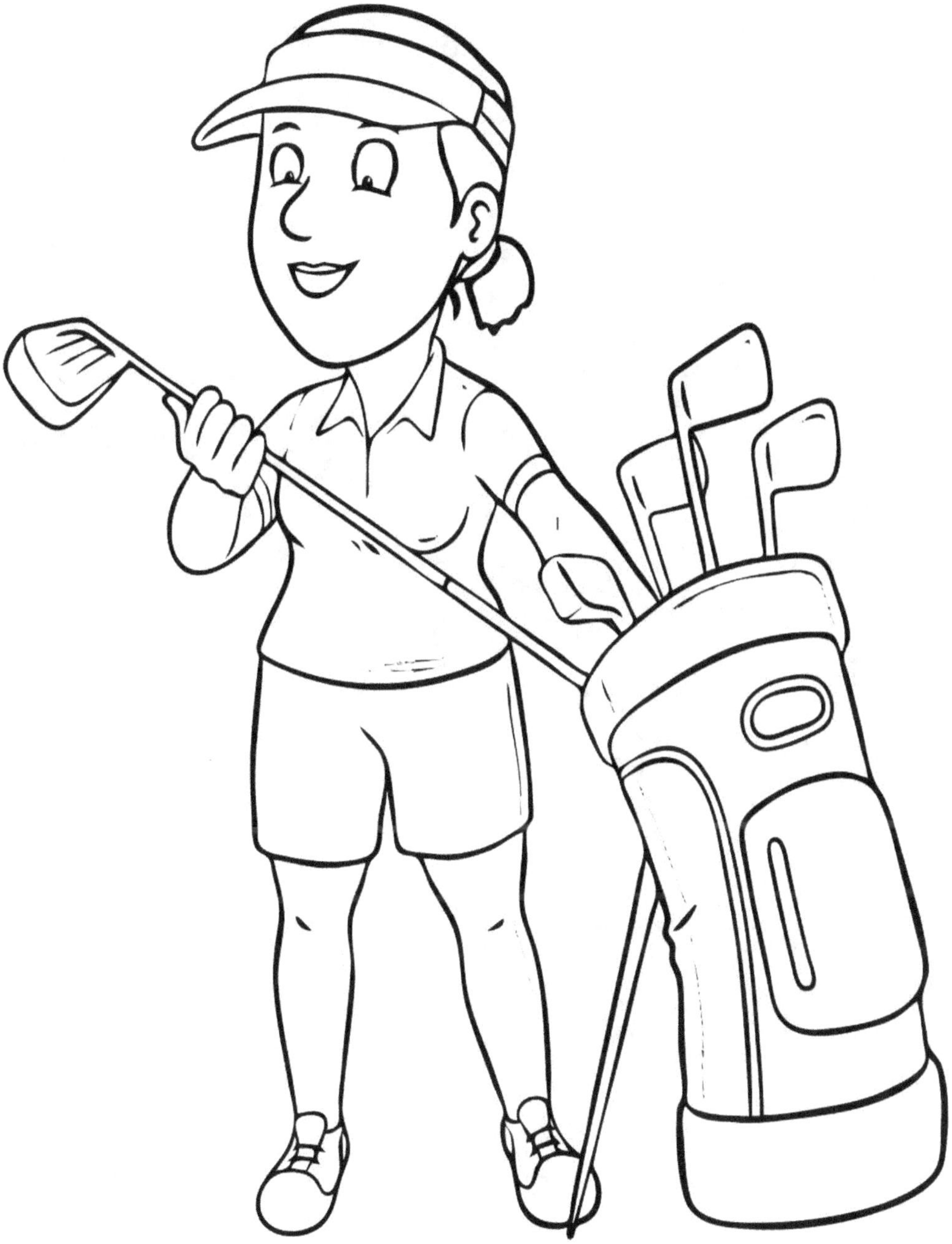

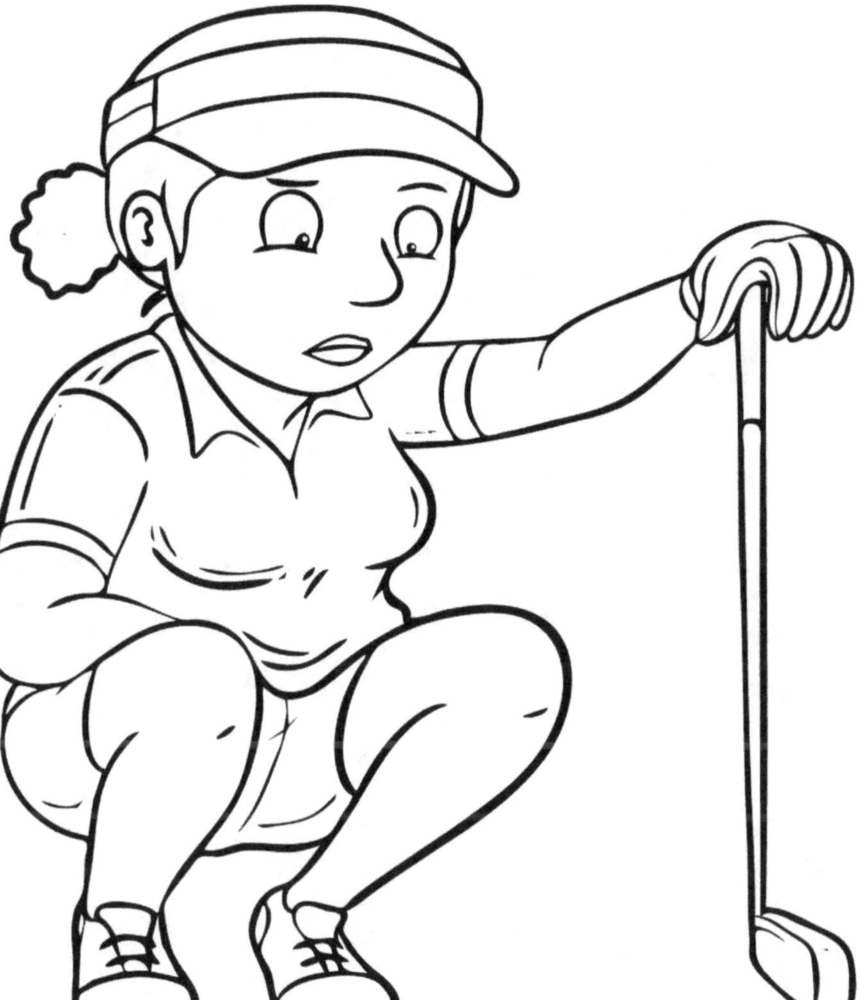

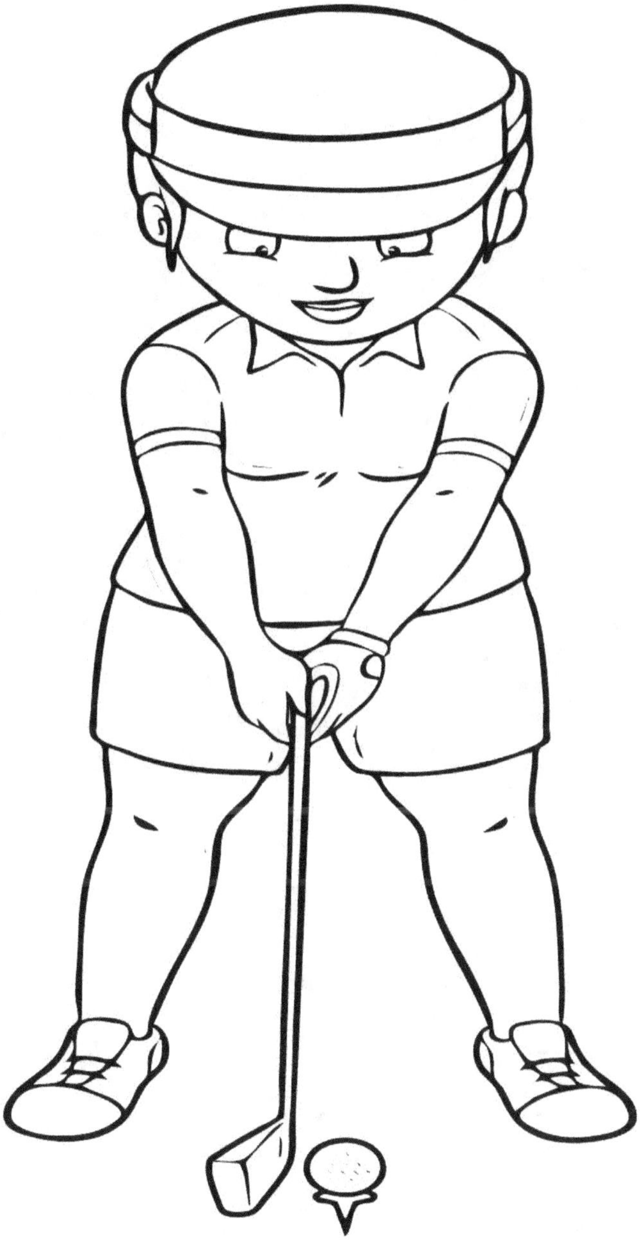

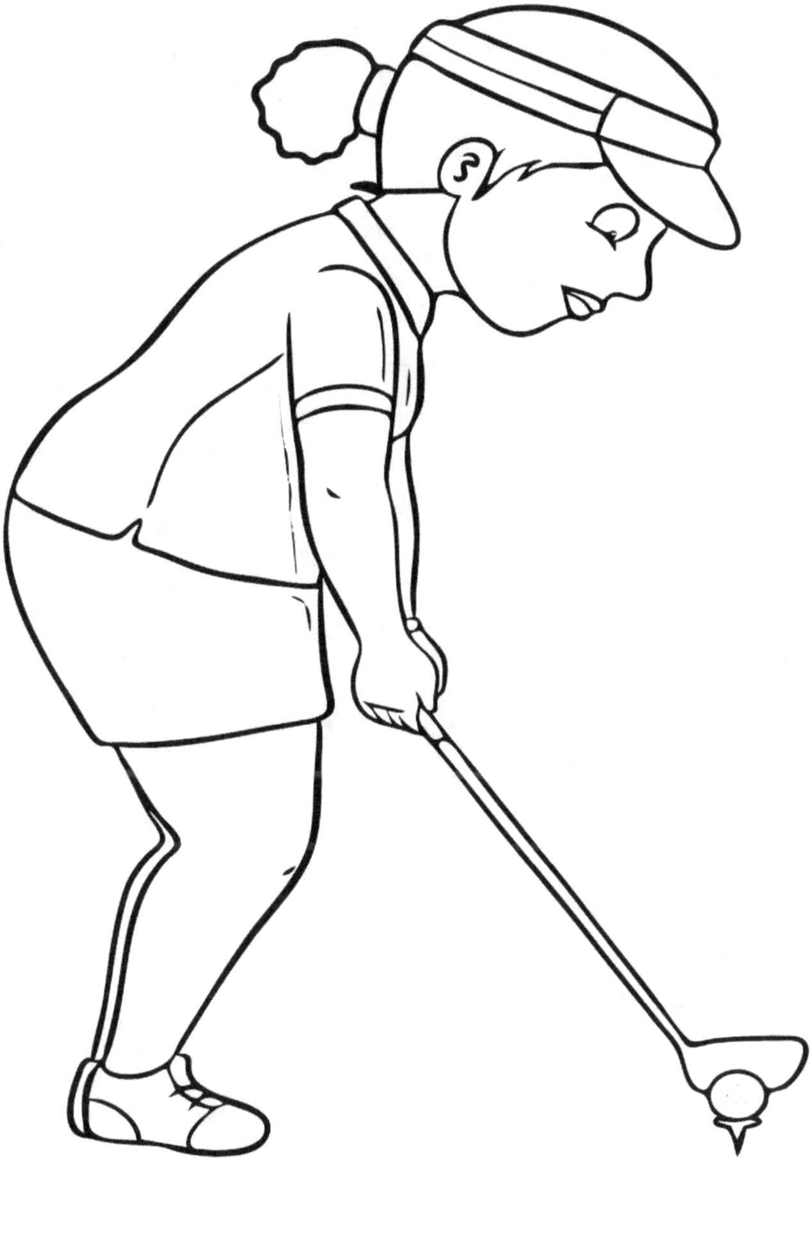

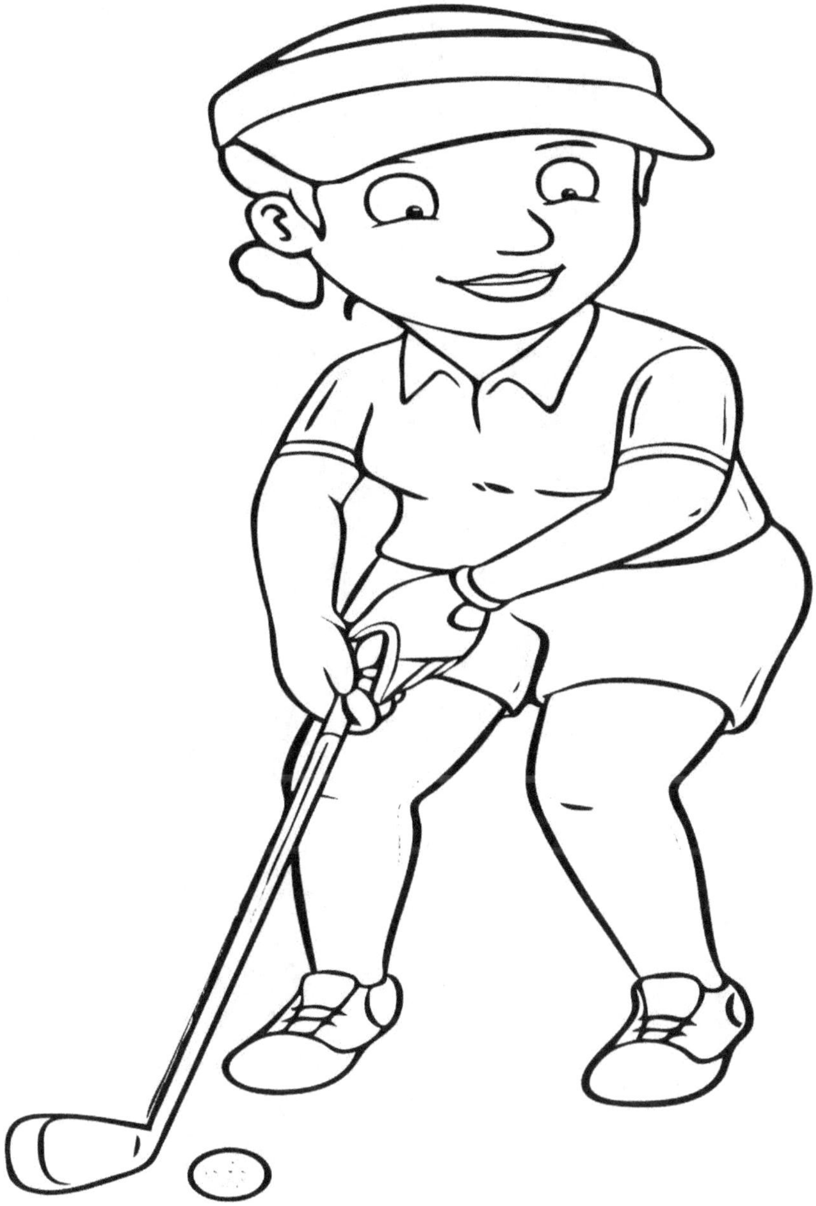

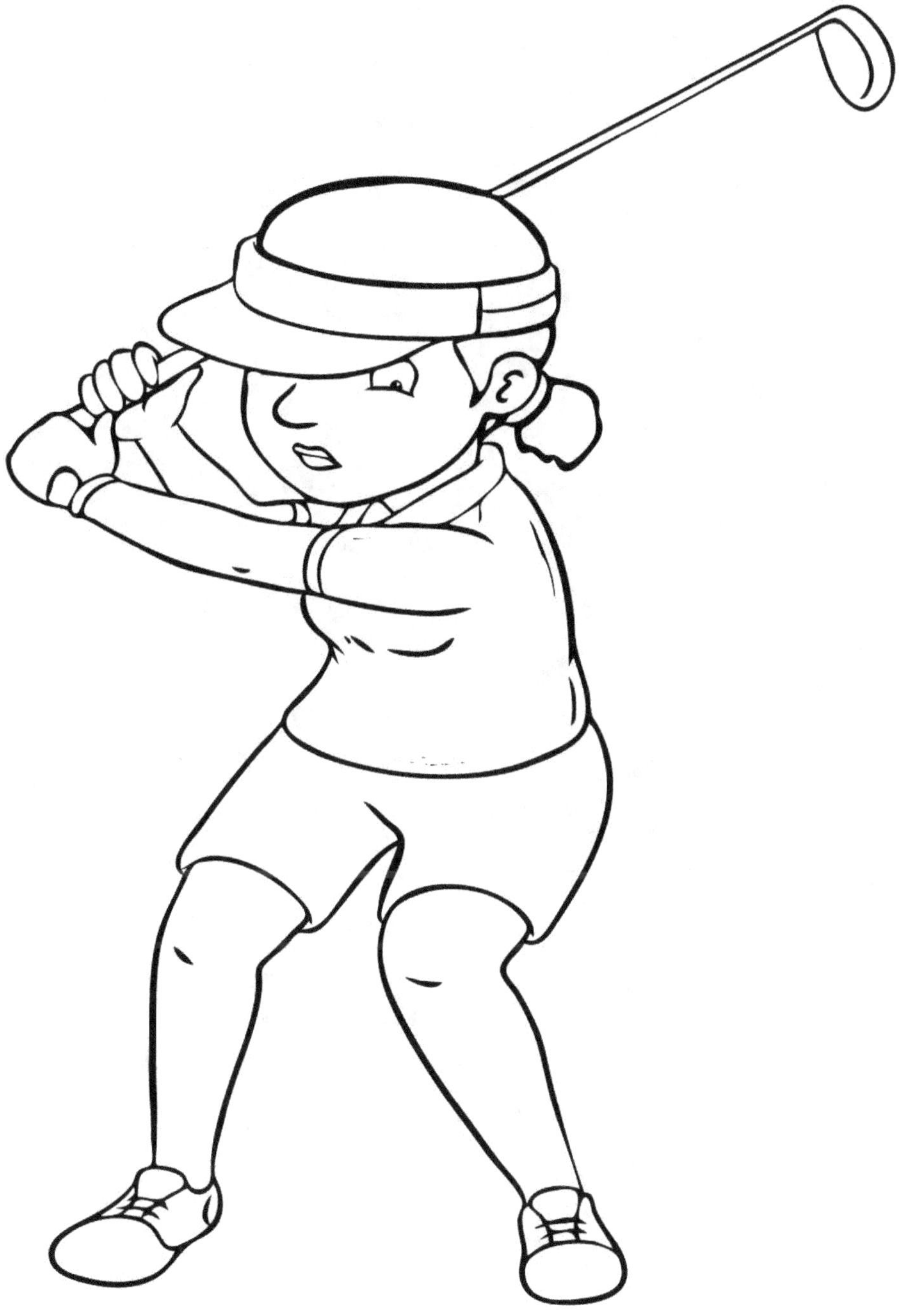

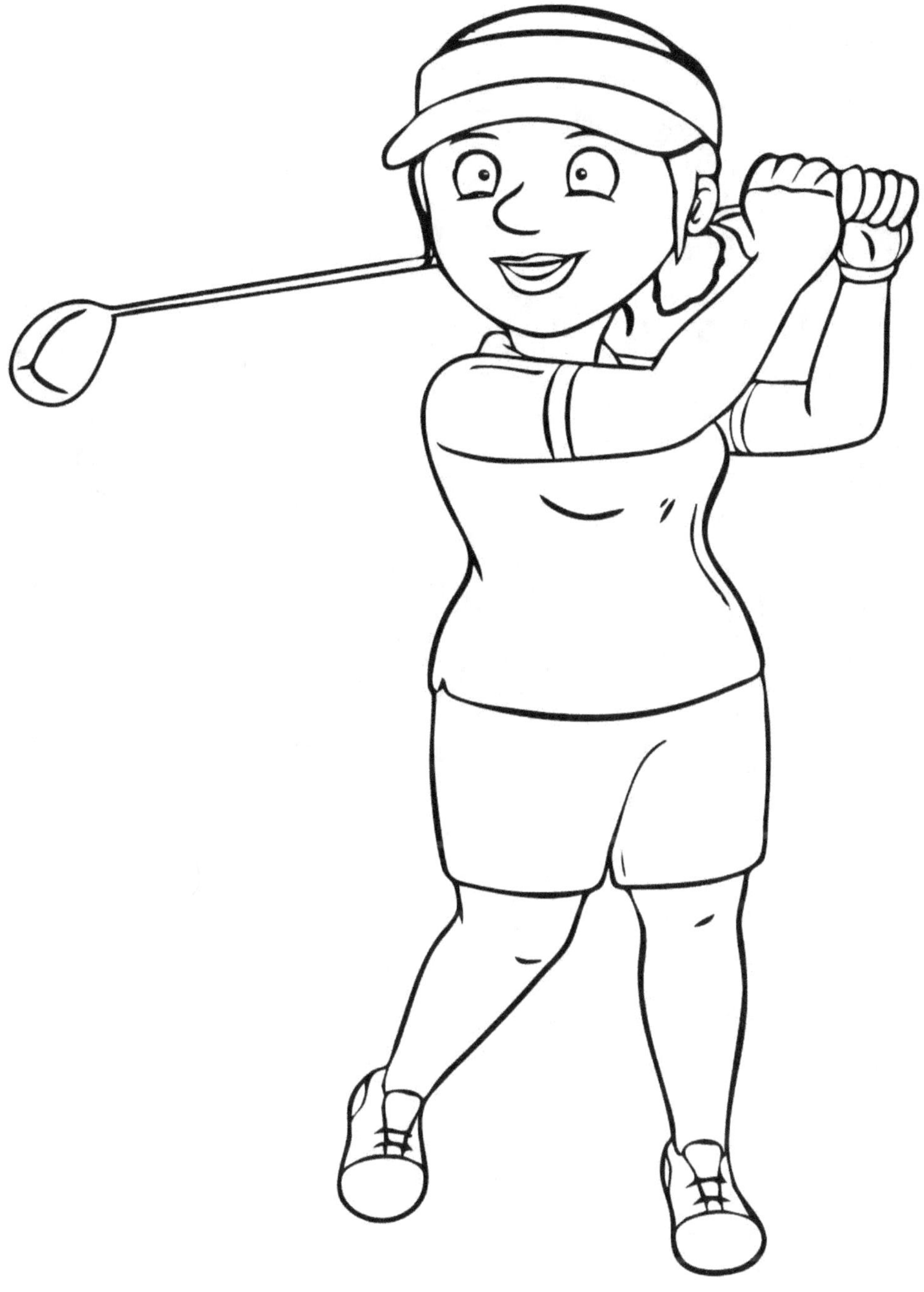

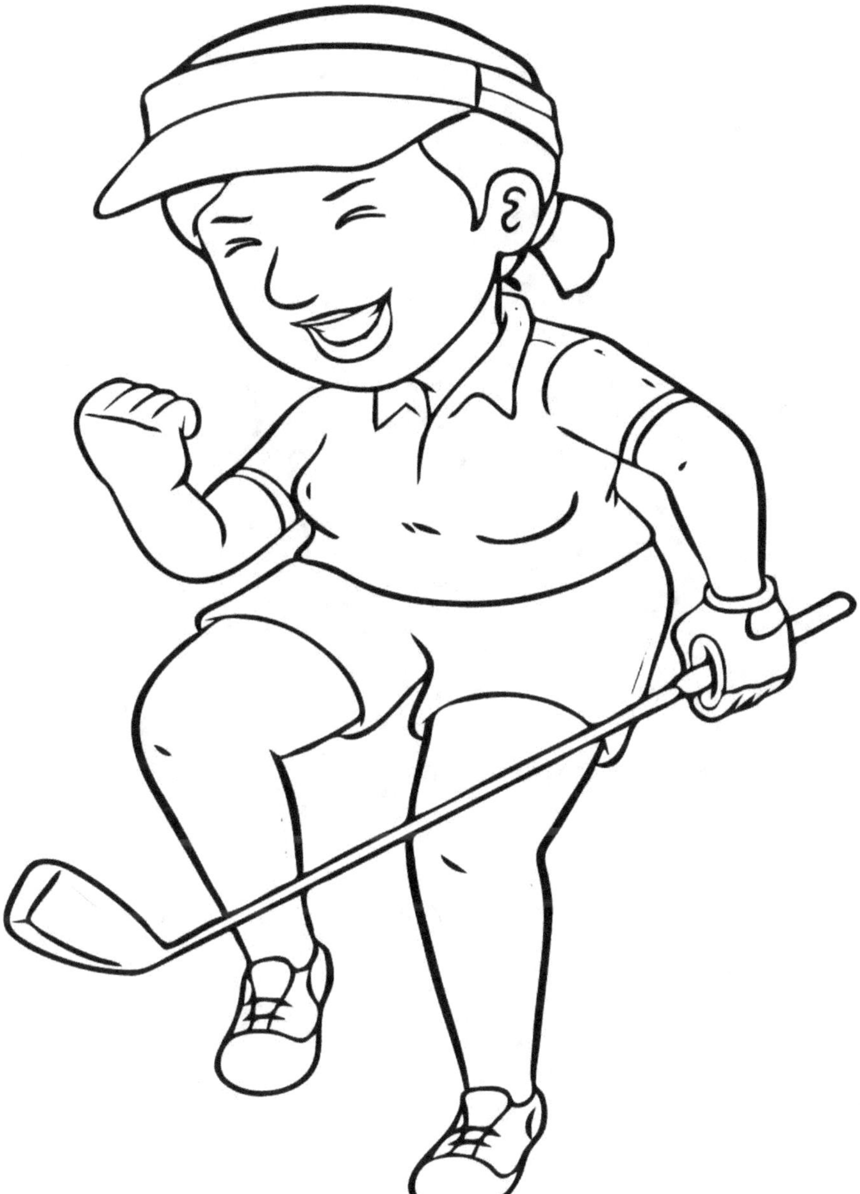

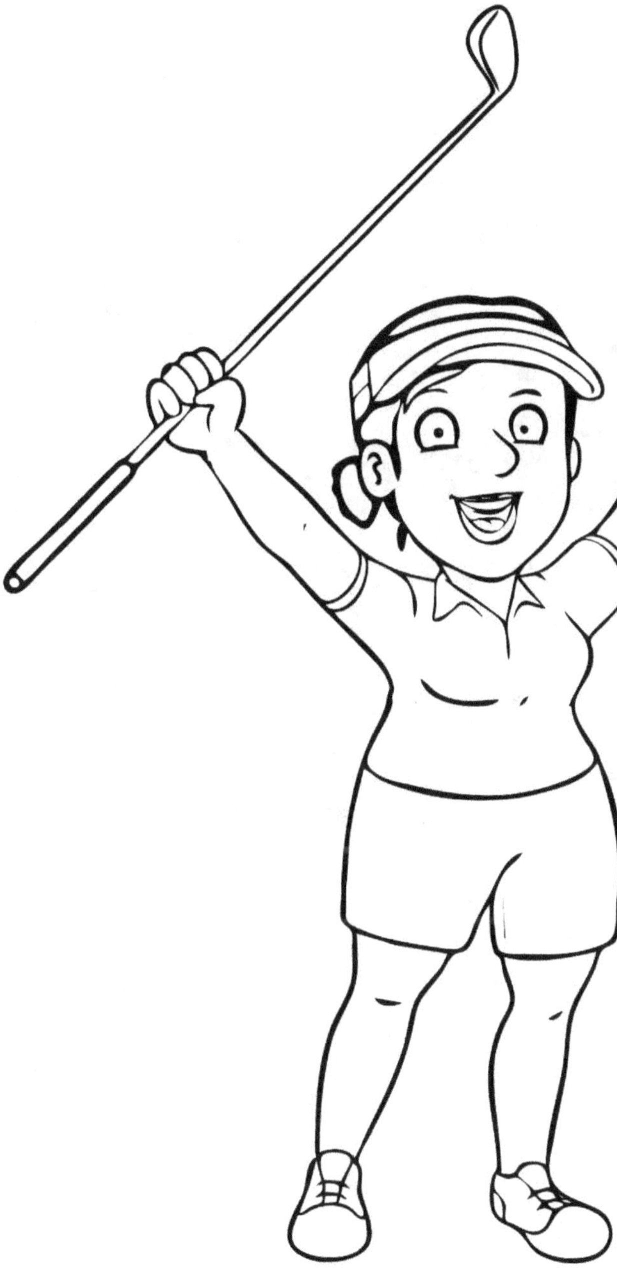

www.ingramcontent.com/pod-product-compliance
Lightning Source LLC
Chambersburg PA
CBHW081406170526
45166CB00010B/3230
9781519331830